Original title:
The Case of the Curious Quest

Author: Gideon Shaw
ISBN HARDBACK: 978-9916-90-294-3
ISBN PAPERBACK: 978-9916-90-295-0

A Quest Beyond the Known

In shadows deep, where whispers roam,
A path unfolds, calling us home.
With stars above as guiding light,
We chase the dreams that fill the night.

Through valleys wide and mountains steep,
The secrets call, their promises keep.
Each step we take, a story sewn,
In quest beyond the great unknown.

Obscured Adventures Await

Beneath the fog, the treasure lies,
In muted tones beneath the skies.
With every turn, a chance to find,
A world of wonder intertwined.

The maps are worn, but hearts are wild,
Seeking paths like a curious child.
Through tangled trees, the whispers play,
Obscured adventures lead the way.

The Riddles of the Fabled Lands

In ancient tomes, the tales are spun,
Of battles lost and victories won.
Each riddle posed, a key to doors,
Unlocking magic on distant shores.

The winds of fate twist through the air,
As we decipher with utmost care.
Each line we read, a thread we weave,
In fabled lands, we dare believe.

Treasures of the Heart's Expedition

Through golden fields where wildflowers dance,
We seek the truths that spark romance.
With every heartbeat, every breath,
We gather treasures that defy death.

The glimmering gems of joy and tears,
Reflect the light of all our years.
In this expedition, souls unite,
Finding diamonds in the starlit night.

Cartography of the Soul's Desire

Mapping the stars that guide my heart,
Each point a longing, a brand new start.
In whispered dreams, I trace the map,
Navigating shadows, feeling the gap.

With ink of hope, I draw my way,
Across the night, through night and day.
Every curve a wish, every line a need,
To follow the path where my soul can feed.

Pathways to the Echoing Beyond

Through valleys deep and mountains high,
I chase the echoes where spirits lie.
Each step a rhythm, a pulse, a song,
In whispers of silence, I know I belong.

The trails unwinding, in twilight’s grace,
Lead me to shadows, to time and space.
With every heartbeat, mysteries unfold,
In the echoing silence, the stories told.

Woven Tales of the Wanderlust

Threads of adventure stitched with care,
In tapestry moments, memories share.
From distant lands to familiar shores,
Each tale a treasure that endlessly pours.

With every journey, a life to weave,
In colors vibrant, I choose to believe.
The fabric of dreams, both soft and bold,
Woven in stories, eternally told.

Frequencies of Forgotten Pathways

In whispers of grass, in rustling leaves,
The frequencies hum where the spirit believes.
Lost in the echoes of paths once clear,
I tune my heart to the sounds I hear.

Each step on this journey, a note in the air,
Reminding me gently that I must dare.
To walk these forgotten, to dance in the mist,
In the symphony of life, I cannot resist.

Mysteries Beneath the Moonlight

Amidst the shadows soft and pale,
Whispers dance upon the vale,
Silent secrets, hidden schemes,
Carried softly on moonlit beams.

Figures shift in silvered glow,
Unravel tales that none may know,
Veils of night cloak every sound,
Where dreams and truths are tightly bound.

In the depths, a lover’s sigh,
Echoes where the owls fly,
Moonlit paths weave through the trees,
Drawing hearts into the breeze.

What lies beyond this twilight fare?
Glimmers of hope and whispered prayer,
Beneath the stars, we roam so free,
In mysteries, we find the key.

Reflections of the Arcane Voyage

Across the waves, the shadows shift,
Carrying tales, a timeless gift,
Ancient mariners, lost at sea,
Charting realms beyond the spree.

Mirrored light on water's crest,
Guiding dreams to endless quest,
Winds of fate and tides of change,
In this dance, the world feels strange.

Eerie whispers fill the air,
Boundless ventures, fate laid bare,
Stars align with fateful grace,
Onward through this vast embrace.

At every dawn, a new refrain,
Echoing the call of grain,
Navigating through dark and light,
We journey on, beyond the night.

Footprints in the Twilight

Softest echoes where the shadows blend,
Mark the paths where memories wend,
Fading traces on the silent earth,
Tell the stories of our worth.

Crimson skies as daylight fades,
Footfalls linger in distant glades,
Whispers rise from the evening chill,
Time stands still on the old hill.

With every step, a breath of night,
Guides us onward, eyes alight,
Hidden truths in twilight's grasp,
We hold the stars within our clasp.

Each footprint tells of where we've been,
Carving paths through the unseen,
As darkness falls, we find our way,
In twilight's glow, forever stay.

Labyrinths of Lost Dreams

Within the maze of whispered fears,
Echoes of past, laughter, tears,
Wandering through each twisting lane,
Loved and lost, the joy, the pain.

Flickering lights in corners dim,
Promises fade, hopes grow slim,
Desires etched in fleeting time,
Chasing shadows, seeking rhyme.

In every turn, a silent plea,
For solace found in memory,
Yet in the dark, a spark ignites,
Lighting paths with soft delights.

In labyrinths, we seek, we find,
The dreams that linger, intertwined,
Through winding ways, our hearts still yearn,
For every tale, a chance to learn.

Mystical Paths of the Heart

Wandering through shadows, whispers unfold,
Each turn holds a secret, in stories untold.
Hearts dance with the moonlight, soft and bright,
Guiding lost spirits through the velvet night.

In echoes of laughter, dreams take their flight,
On paths woven softly, by stars' gentle light.
Love’s gentle caress, like a warm, tender breeze,
Awakens the magic that puts the soul at ease.

Journeying Through the Depths of Wonder

A river of starlight flows deep in the mind,
Where thoughts swim like fish, elusive yet kind.
The depths hold their secrets, both ancient and new,
Beckoning wanderers to plunge, to renew.

With every step forward, horizons expand,
Where questions like seeds fall upon fertile land.
Curiosity stirs in the depths of the soul,
As wonders emerge, making fragments feel whole.

Errant Thoughts on a Winding Trail

The path twists and turns, in meandering ways,
Each thought a small pebble, in sunshine it plays.
With laughter that echoes, in the leaves overhead,
And whispers of wisdom, where angels have tread.

Beneath the tall pines, the air thick with dreams,
Mind's eye opens wide, to a world bursting at seams.
Errant thoughts drift like clouds in the sky,
Painting the canvas as moments pass by.

Traces of the Unexplored

Footprints in the sand lead to worlds yet to claim,
Every twist and turn, a new glimpse of the same.
Hidden doors beckon, with mysteries inside,
In places untouched, where imagination hides.

The silence speaks volumes, in echoes of time,
Every story lingers, like a well-versed rhyme.
With courage as compass, the heart starts to soar,
Unraveling life's tapestry, yearning for more.

Glimmers of Distant Shores

Whispers of waves roll to the sand,
Under the sun, dreams stretch and expand.
The horizon glows with a golden hue,
Each moment beckons, a promise anew.

Seagulls dance in the azure sky,
Echoes of freedom as they glide high.
Shells tell stories of long ago,
Time's gentle touch in the ebb and flow.

Discoveries at the Edge of Mystery

In the shadows where secrets hide,
Curiosity sparks a relentless tide.
With every step, wonders unfold,
Truths waiting, daring and bold.

The path we tread, a winding maze,
Each corner turned, igniting a blaze.
Unveiling depths, we learn to see,
The beauty woven in life's tapestry.

Footprints in the Realm of Curiosity

Each footprint left on unmarked ground,
A quest for knowledge, joy profound.
Questions linger, dancing in the air,
Every answer leads us to dare.

With wonder as our guiding star,
We journey forth, though near or far.
Through valleys deep and mountains tall,
Curiosity's call, we heed its thrall.

The Odyssey of Hidden Truths

Beyond the veil where shadows play,
Lies a journey that lights our way.
With courage deep, we seek and strive,
To understand the truths that thrive.

Through storms of doubt we brave the night,
In pursuit of wisdom, our guiding light.
Each unveiled secret, a step in grace,
In the odyssey, we find our place.

Fables of the Fearless Traveler

In a land where shadows creep,
A traveler wanders, thoughts to keep.
With every step, a story unfolds,
In whispered legends, the heart beholds.

Mountains rise, the skies are vast,
Each challenge met, a spell is cast.
With courage bright and dreams aglow,
The fearless traveler dares to go.

Through valleys deep and rivers wide,
Every truth is both a guide.
With open eyes, the world reveals,
A tapestry spun of raw appeals.

So heed the tales, let them ignite,
The spirit's spark, a guiding light.
For every journey, great or small,
Is a fable waiting to enthrall.

Beyond the Boundaries of Belief

They travel far where few may tread,
With questions lingering in each thread.
Beyond the walls where doubts confine,
A search for truths, both bold and divine.

In realms where reason starts to bend,
They meet the unknown, a faithful friend.
With eyes wide open to the skies,
They learn to see through mystic eyes.

The stars above, they weave their tales,
Of courage found when logic fails.
Each whispered thought, each silent plea,
Brings forth the magic in destiny.

For in the heart where dreams collide,
Beyond belief, the spirits guide.
A journey sparked by endless quest,
In the unknown, they find their rest.

Questing Through Candlelit Adventures

In twilight's glow, the candles burn,
A flickering flame, a world to learn.
With shadows dancing on stone-cold walls,
A whispered secret in twilight calls.

Maps unfold with tales of old,
Adventures rich, the air feels bold.
Each step a journey, heart aligned,
With quests to seek and treasures to find.

Through labyrinths of dreams and fears,
Into the night, where time adheres.
Candlelit paths, they softly weave,
In stories told, so hard to leave.

For every flame that sparks delight,
Holds dreams awakened in the night.
In candlelight, horizons gleam,
A quest ignited, a daring dream.

Signs of the Hidden Pilgrimage

Beneath the veil, the signs appear,
Whispers of journeys, crystal clear.
With every step the heart will know,
The path unfolds, where dreams will flow.

Through forests deep and mountains high,
Each token found beneath the sky.
In sacred spaces, wisdom grows,
In silence heard, the spirit knows.

The footprints left, a tale to tell,
Of hidden realms where travelers dwell.
Each sigh and glance, a compass true,
The pilgrimage calls to me and you.

So heed the signs, the ancient lore,
In every heartbeat, seek for more.
For those who wander ever free,
Discover the depths of destiny.

Pathways to the Uncharted

Beneath the shade of ancient trees,
Whispers of journeys dance on the breeze.
Footprints lead where few have tread,
Into the realms where fears are shed.

Echoes of dreams beneath the stars,
Crickets sing in chorus, the night is ours.
With every step, the fog now clears,
We're chasing wonders through our fears.

Paths entwine in a twilight glow,
With secrets waiting to bestow.
Adventure calls in the quiet night,
Guiding spirits with soft, sweet light.

Flights of Fancy in the Wild Unknown

Wings unfurl into the skies,
A dance of colors, swift and wise.
Through forests deep and mountains high,
Dreams take flight, like birds they sigh.

With every gale that lifts us near,
We feast on freedom, shed our fear.
Tales of wonder in every breeze,
Shores of mystery lie to seize.

In tangled vines, we write our stories,
With laughter, light, and hidden glories.
A tapestry of chance and fate,
In endless journeys, we celebrate.

Glimmers Along the Forgotten Route

Along the path where shadows creep,
Glimmers of hope arise from deep.
With lanterns lit on darkened trails,
We walk through tales where silence sails.

Each rustling leaf sings whispered lore,
Of dreams embraced and quests galore.
In every turn, we find our way,
Through hidden realms where spirits play.

The night's embrace, a guide so wise,
Illuminates the starlit skies.
With hearts aglow, we journey forth,
The magic calls, igniting worth.

The Search for Forgotten Echoes

In ancient halls where voices fade,
We seek the tales that time has made.
Footsteps linger on dusty floors,
Whispers haunt through open doors.

With every echo, a story flows,
Revelations found where the river goes.
Memories woven in silence deep,
Awakened dreams, no longer sleep.

In the heart of shadows, light breaks free,
Connecting threads of you and me.
Through past's embrace, we search for truth,
In forgotten echoes lies our youth.

Spirited Away Through the Mist

In the morning mist, whispers roam,
Eyes are half-closed, dreams feel like home.
Footsteps echo on paths unseen,
Guided by shadows, lost in between.

Waves of silence dance 'round the trees,
Breaths of the ancients carried by breeze.
Colors dissolve as the daylight fades,
Secrets of nature in twilight cascades.

Ventures in the Veil of the Unknown

A world of wonders awaits to explore,
Beyond the horizon, where spirits soar.
With each daring step, the heart beats fast,
Chasing the echoes of dreams unsurpassed.

Voices of starlight whisper and weave,
In the tapestry of night, we believe.
Through valleys of silence, time unravels,
Mapping our journeys on winding travels.

Riddles Resolved in the Wild

Amidst the tangled roots and thorny trails,
Nature's riddles paint stories and tales.
With every rustle, an answer unfolds,
Secrets of life in the wilderness told.

A flicker of light in the shadowed glen,
Guides lost souls back to where they've been.
Trust in the journey, the path will reveal,
The mysteries hidden beneath each appeal.

Curiosities of the Horizon's End

Chasing the sun where the sky meets the sea,
Curiosities spark wild, untamed and free.
With every horizon, a beckoning call,
Whispers of wonder echo through all.

As twilight descends, the colors collide,
In the dance of the stars, dreams coincide.
Infinite stories lie just out of reach,
At the edge of the world, the heart learns to teach.

Adventures Beyond the Known Skies

Above the clouds where eagles soar,
A world awaits, forever more.
With dreams that touch the stars so bright,
We chase the dawn, embracing light.

In whispers of the evening breeze,
We find the secrets held in trees.
Each journey leads to lands unknown,
Where courage blooms and seeds are sown.

Through valleys deep and mountains high,
We'll paint our stories in the sky.
Together we will chart the maps,
Unfold the wings, elude the traps.

With every step, the wild calls out,
To chase the magic, free from doubt.
In adventures bold, we'll heed the song,
And write our tale where we belong.

Sagas of Shifting Shadows

In twilight's grasp, the shadows sway,
Tales of old, in shades of gray.
Whispers linger on the night,
Echoes of past, fading light.

Each figure dances with a tale,
Of love and loss, of dreams so frail.
Within the mist, their fates entwine,
In every shadow, a story shines.

The moonlight weaves through ancient trees,
Telling tales on the evening breeze.
Fragments lost in time's embrace,
Sagas of life, we must retrace.

From dusk till dawn, the stories unfold,
In hidden realms, where hearts are bold.
With every breath, the shadows speak,
Of strength and courage, our souls seek.

The Allure of the Undiscovered Realms

Beyond the horizon, where dreams reside,
Untouched landscapes, a thrilling ride.
With each step into the vast unknown,
We seek the wonders yet to be shown.

In valleys hidden from the light,
The allure calls, glowing and bright.
Mysteries steeped in ancient lore,
Open the doors to a brand-new shore.

Through forests deep and rivers wide,
Our spirits soar, with nature as guide.
Each heartbeat matches the wild song,
Echoing truths where we belong.

Together, let's traverse the wide seas,
Chasing the trails of the gentle breeze.
In these realms where adventure gleams,
We live the magic of our dreams.

Scavenger Hunt of the Heart

With every glance, where eyes collide,
A treasure map for hearts to guide.
In laughter shared beneath the sky,
We search for love, our spirits high.

Each moment's gem, a fleeting glance,
In heart's array, we find our chance.
The little things that make us whole,
Are whispers woven in the soul.

Through winding paths and hidden nooks,
We seek the volumes written in books.
With every step, we learn the part,
Of this grand hunt, the scavenger's heart.

In memories made, the treasures gleam,
Stringing the pearls of a vivid dream.
With open hearts, we chase the art,
Of finding joy, our boundless heart.

Trails of Unseen Wonders

In the whispering woods, shadows play,
Beneath the arching trees, dreams sway.
Every path diverges, secrets unfold,
Stories of the heart, waiting to be told.

Rivers of silence and mountains high,
Where the eagles soar and the spirits fly.
Nature's canvas paints a sacred hue,
In the dance of the dusk, the world feels new.

The Riddle of the Uncharted Realm

Mystic lands call to the brave and bold,
Whispers of secrets in legends old.
Maps written in stars, yet lost in time,
Untwist the riddles, let reason climb.

Oceans of thought, cliffs of the mind,
Winds of the unknown, leave doubts behind.
Each journey starts with a single breath,
In the heart of the quest, we conquer death.

Fables of a Timeless Adventure

Under the moonlight, stories ignite,
Fables woven in the fabric of night.
Legends of courage, woven with grace,
Each lesson learned, time cannot erase.

From ancient scrolls, wisdom takes flight,
Transforming the mundane to pure delight.
In the echoes of ages, we find our way,
Creating new fables with each passing day.

Chronicles of Lost Horizons

Beyond the horizon, dreams take their stand,
Maps of the heart trace the unseen land.
In the glow of the dawn, paths intertwine,
Echoes of destinies, boldly align.

The tales of the lost, whisper through trees,
Songs of remembrance carried by breeze.
In every sunset, the past finds its voice,
In shadows of twilight, we make our choice.

Shadows of the Unfamiliar Road

Through shadows cast by midnight's glow,
Unfamiliar paths begin to show.
Each step a whisper of the night,
A journey cloaked in silver light.

With every twist, the heart beats fast,
Memories linger, shadows cast.
Beneath the stars, the questions rise,
What lies ahead, beneath the skies?

Footprints fading, lost in time,
Echoes drift like a distant chime.
The road ahead, a secret bound,
In every silence, dreams profound.

Yet courage sparks within the soul,
To face the night and seek the whole.
For in the dark, the truth will glow,
Illuminating the unknown road.

Tales from the Treasured Horizon

At dawn's embrace, the stories wake,
Whispers ride the gentle lake.
Each tale stitched with golden thread,
From distant lands where dreams are fed.

The horizon beckons with a song,
Legends of where we all belong.
Through valleys vast and mountains tall,
The call of wanderlust for all.

In every heart, a treasure lies,
A map unfolded 'neath the skies.
With every step, we chase the light,
To find our place in the vast night.

So gather close, let stories flow,
From cherished pasts, our spirits grow.
For in these tales, we find our start,
The treasures held within the heart.

The Veiled Pursuit

In shadowed corners of our dreams,
A pursuit veiled in moonlit beams.
We chase the whispers of the night,
Seeking truth within the fright.

The world obscured by mists of doubt,
A journey paved with silent shout.
In every corner, shadows weave,
A dance of what we dare believe.

Yet light breaks through the heavy gloom,
Creating space for hearts to bloom.
As veils of fear begin to fall,
We rise again, we heed the call.

With courage stitched into our seams,
We venture forth to chase the dreams.
For in the veiled pursuit we find,
A strength that binds both heart and mind.

Odyssey of the Unlikely Seekers

With mismatched maps and uneven shoes,
Unlikely seekers refuse to lose.
Their journey long, yet filled with hope,
Through rugged paths and twisted slope.

In every smile, the world expands,
Together brave, they make their stands.
Through storms and trials, they hold on tight,
An odyssey born of shared delight.

Each story told brings light anew,
In every heart, a spark breaks through.
Against the odds, they stand as one,
Their search for truth has just begun.

So let the winds of change now blow,
As seekers gather, spirits glow.
For in their quest, the world ignites,
An odyssey of hopeful sights.

Secrets of the Wandering Spirit

In shadows where whispers weave,
Lost tales that only night can conceive.
The moon hides secrets, soft and deep,
In the silence where dreams quietly creep.

Footsteps dance on paths untold,
Where courage blooms, and fears grow bold.
A flicker of light guides the way,
To lands where the spirit longs to stay.

Each breath a story, each gaze a spell,
The wandering spirit knows it well.
Through valleys of hope and mountains of sighs,
The truth of the heart never truly dies.

With every turn, the essence unfolds,
In the canvas of night, a journey holds.
Embrace the unknown, let the wander reign,
For secrets are treasures buried in the grain.

The Journey to the Whimsical Unknown

A cart of dreams rolls down the lane,
With laughter echoing, free from pain.
Colors twirl in the afternoon light,
As we dance with shadows, spirits in flight.

Through forests where the wildflowers sing,
The air is thick with the magic of spring.
Each step we take, a story anew,
To the whimsical lands where wonders accrue.

Upon the lakes where reflections blend,
We chase the horizons, our hearts transcend.
With each heartbeat, the adventure calls,
In the unexpected, joy freely falls.

Let not the mundane dull our bright spark,
For within the unknown, we leave our mark.
With eyes wide open, let us embrace,
The journey ahead, a fantastical place.

Echoes and Elysium

In the vale where echoes softly play,
Memories linger, glimmering grey.
The whispers of love, the sighs of the past,
In the heartbeats of time, they forever last.

Elysium calls, a haven so bright,
Underneath the stars, a magical sight.
In gardens where laughter is woven with grace,
We dance with the shadows, lost in space.

Each murmur a promise, each glance a song,
In the tapestry of life, we all belong.
Though the echoes may fade in the soft whispering breeze,
The essence of joy is in moments like these.

So let us wander through this twilight embrace,
Finding solace and beauty in time and space.
For echoes and Elysium are one and the same,
In the heart of the world, love is the flame.

Strangers in the Light of Adventure

Amidst the glow, we wander forth,
Two souls aligned, yet worlds apart.
With every step, a story sings,
In the whispering wind, adventure springs.

Beneath the stars, our fears dissolve,
What lies ahead, we can't resolve.
Each laugh exchanged, a thread we weave,
In the tapestry of the eve.

Through twisted paths, we find our way,
New friends unveiled in shadows play.
In moments stolen, we dare to dream,
Together, a flickering, united beam.

With hearts ablaze, we chase the night,
As strangers glow in adventure's light.
The journey calls, a siren's song,
In every heartbeat, we belong.

The Allure of the Unknown Voyage

On waves of change, we set to sail,
Where maps are lost, and dreams prevail.
The horizon beckons, a siren's call,
Into the depths where shadows fall.

With every gust, our spirits rise,
Unfurling dreams like open skies.
The compass spins, a guiding force,
In this dance of fate, we find our course.

The stars align, their secrets keep,
In whispered tales of oceans deep.
We leave behind the known and try,
To soar on wings, to dare and fly.

The moonlight casts its gentle glow,
In the vast unknown, our spirits flow.
As tides embrace, we forge ahead,
In the allure of where we've not yet tread.

Searching for Fragments of Reality

In shattered dreams, we seek the light,
Fragments of truth in the quiet night.
With curious hearts, we roam the vast,
To piece together echoes of the past.

Through whispered winds and fading stars,
We chase the ghosts of our own scars.
In every shadow, a moment finds,
The beauty hidden in fractured minds.

Among the ruins, we dare to tread,
The stories linger where once they bled.
In every sigh, a glimpse remains,
Of lives once draped in joyous strains.

We gather hope from the scattered light,
In fragments, we find our shared delight.
For every piece, though torn apart,
Is part of the whole within the heart.

The Map of Unimagined Paths

In pages worn, a secret lays,
The map of dreams in a timeless haze.
With every line, a trail begins,
To hidden lands where wonder spins.

Through valleys deep and mountains high,
We trace our hopes beneath the sky.
Each step we take, a daring flight,
On paths that shimmer, pure delight.

In distant whispers, tales unfold,
Of journeys bright and legends bold.
The compass swings with untold chance,
Inviting us to join the dance.

With open hearts, we step outside,
To journeys vast, our spirits wide.
The map unwinds, a challenge gleams,
As we uncover our wildest dreams.

Turning Pages of Wandering Tales

In the hushed glow of twilight's grace,
New worlds unfold in a quiet space.
Each line a step, each word a sigh,
Stories of wanderers drifting by.

With every turn, the whispers call,
Adventures beckon, both great and small.
Footprints linger on pages worn,
Ink of the past, a tale reborn.

Dreams entwined in a tapestry bright,
Mapping journeys through day and night.
In pages turned, the heart can soar,
A dance of legends, forevermore.

The Allure of Forgotten Trails

Where wildflowers sway in the golden sun,
Old paths reveal where the river runs.
Footsteps echo in the softest earth,
Each trail retells of joy and mirth.

Beneath the trees, whispers of the past,
Secrets linger, shadows cast.
In the silence, stories sleep,
Of those who wandered, and memories deep.

The air is sweet with the scent of pine,
Nature's canvas, a grand design.
Each corner turned, a beauty unfolds,
The allure of trails that time holds.

With every step, a bond is made,
In wild embrace, fears start to fade.
The heart finds solace, the spirit sails,
In the sweet allure of forgotten trails.

Whispers of the Wandering Path

Beneath the stars, a journey begun,
Barefoot stories in moonlight spun.
The winding road, a gentle guide,
Whispers beckon from the other side.

Every breeze carries tales untold,
Magic dances in the night so bold.
With hush of leaves, the path reveals,
Hidden truths that time conceals.

In the shadows, the heart takes flight,
Chasing dreams into the night.
Each footfall paints a vivid scene,
Guided by whisper, soft and keen.

Among the trees, a spirit roams,
Finding solace in nature's poems.
The wandering path leads to the soul,
In whispers sweet, we become whole.

Secrets of the Starlit Journey

Under a canvas of twinkling light,
Dreamers roam through the vast, deep night.
Each star a guide, a shimmering sign,
Revealing secrets, both yours and mine.

The universe hums a gentle tune,
As we traverse beneath the moon.
With every glance at the skies so wide,
We find our truths in the cosmic tide.

In the quiet hours, the world transforms,
A tapestry of fate in swirling forms.
Every heartbeat echoes through the dark,
Illuminated by a brilliant spark.

With stories woven in celestial thread,
We wander forth where the stars have led.
Through whispered magic, we shall roam,
In the secrets of the starlit dome.

Whispers in the Winding Woods

In the heart of the woods, where the moonlight gleams,
Nature speaks softly, feeding our dreams.
Leaves rustle gently, a comforting sound,
As shadows dance lightly on the cool, damp ground.

Wisps of adventure cling to the air,
Lost in the whispers, we wander with care.
Branches arch overhead, like a welcoming door,
In the embrace of the woods, we long to explore.

Fairies and fireflies play hide and seek,
With stories of old that the night seems to speak.
Each step a promise, each pause a delight,
In the magical woods, we're lost in the night.

So follow the path where the shadows reside,
Trust in the whispers, let your heart be your guide.
For the winding woods hold secrets untold,
In their embrace, we find treasures of gold.

Echoes of an Enigmatic Journey

On roads less traveled, stories unfold,
Echoes of voices from ages of old.
Footsteps like whispers guide us along,
In the dance of the present, they sing us a song.

Winding through valleys with mysteries deep,
Secrets held tight, in the silence we keep.
Each turn brings a tale, with colors so bright,
An enigmatic journey, bathed in soft light.

Mountains stand tall, their shadows embrace,
Guiding our spirits through time and space.
With each fleeting moment, we capture the dream,
As echoes resound, like a flowing stream.

So let us wander where the wild things roam,
Each step an adventure, where we find our home.
In the tapestry woven with threads of the past,
The echoes of journeys forever will last.

Secrets Beneath the Starlit Skies

Under the canvas of velvet so wide,
Stars whisper secrets, in silence they bide.
Crickets play music, serenading the night,
While dreams take their flight, igniting the light.

Each twinkle a promise, each flicker a sign,
Drawing us closer to the mysteries divine.
The moon holds a lantern, casting a glow,
Illuminating pathways where hopes gently flow.

In the quiet of night, hearts learn to believe,
In the power of wishes that we dare to weave.
Old stories of stardust filter through time,
Connecting our souls, in rhythm and rhyme.

So let us lie back, in the cool evening air,
And uncover the secrets that twinkle up there.
For beneath the starlit skies, we shall find,
The magic of wonder that dwells in our mind.

Shadows of a Hidden Path

In twilight's embrace, shadows start to play,
Marking the edges of the fading day.
A hidden path beckons, through trees so tall,
Leading us softly, where the nightbirds call.

With each cautious step, mysteries arise,
Veiled in the stillness, beneath starry skies.
Whispers of shadows, secrets they share,
Enticing our hearts, igniting our care.

A flicker of starlight across the dark trail,
Guiding our spirits when the winds begin to wail.
Through the maze of the night, our fears drift away,
As shadows protect and keep loneliness at bay.

So let us wander, let our worries be shed,
Embrace the shadows in the path we tread.
For hidden within, there's a beauty to find,
In the dance of the shadows, our souls become aligned.

The Allure of the Obscured Destination

Beneath the veil of misty dreams,
A path awaits in silent streams.
Whispers softly call my name,
To wander forth, ignite the flame.

Veiled in twilight's gentle grace,
I seek that lost and secret place.
Where shadows dance in furtive play,
And stars reveal the hidden way.

The air is thick with tales untold,
Of treasures that the brave behold.
Each step, a thread in time's design,
A journey forged where fates align.

For in this realm of quiet chance,
I lose myself, begin to dance.
The allure of the unknown beckons,
As heart and spirit find their reckon.

Secrets of the Nighttime Navigator

Beneath the cloak of starry skies,
The navigator gently sighs.
With compass drawn and heart in hand,
He charts the course through shadowed land.

Nocturnal winds whisper their dreams,
In silvered light, the world redeems.
Each constellation shares its lore,
Awakens souls to seek for more.

He listens close to silence deep,
Where ancient echoes gently creep.
Through veils of night and misty haze,
He finds the path, unfurls the maze.

With every star, a guide anew,
The secrets of the night ring true.
In darkened hours, purpose thrives,
As shadows fade, the light arrives.

In Pursuit of the Enigmatic Light

Chasing beams that flicker bright,
I wander forth into the night.
With every step, the thrill ignites,
A dance between the dark and light.

Where twilight whispers tales of old,
In shadows cast, the dreams unfold.
The luminous beckons from afar,
A beacon's call beneath the stars.

Through forests deep and valleys wide,
I follow where secrets abide.
In search of wonders veiled from sight,
In pursuit of that enigmatic light.

As dawn approaches, fleeting grace,
I cherish each enchanting place.
The journey shapes my very soul,
In quest of light, I find my whole.

Echoes of the Expeditionary Souls

With every stride through untamed land,
The echoes of the past command.
In every heart, the fire glows,
As we embrace the journey's throes.

The voices of the brave still breathe,
In rustling leaves and fragrant heave.
Their stories woven into time,
In whispers carried, soft and prime.

Through trials faced and battles won,
Their spirits shine, they are not done.
In every pulse of life anew,
The echoes guide, their wisdom true.

So onward march, expedition's call,
United in our rise or fall.
With echoes strong and souls alight,
We carve our path, embraced by night.

Echoes of Elysian Exploration

In valleys deep where whispers play,
The winds tell tales of yesterday.
With each step forward, dreams take flight,
In the soft glow of fading light.

Amidst the trees where shadows weave,
The heart finds peace, the soul believes.
In every rustle, secrets bloom,
Awakening hope in twilight's room.

The stars align in velvet skies,
Guiding the lost with gentle sighs.
A journey forged in dusk's embrace,
Reveals the magic of this place.

With every echo of footfall near,
Life speaks softly, calm and clear.
In Elysium, where dreams are spun,
A tale unfolds, and we are one.

Enigmas of the Unseen Trail

Through mists that hug the winding path,
Lies a riddle invoking the aftermath.
With every step cloaked in intrigue,
The heart quickens, it starts to league.

Beneath the canopy, secrets lie,
In the dance of shadows, truth meets the eye.
The branches whisper of days untold,
In this wooden realm, the brave are bold.

Footprints linger, fading away,
As the unknown beckons, come what may.
A map drawn by fate, not by hand,
Invites the wanderer to understand.

Each turn unveils new sights unseen,
The journey flows like a mystic dream.
In enigmas forged by nature's grace,
Every moment finds a sacred space.

The Serendipitous Search

Beneath the stars where wishes weave,
A serendipitous path to believe.
With open hearts and spirits bold,
We tread on tales that fate has told.

In laughter shared and moments bright,
Providence shines in the soft moonlight.
As fortunes twist and chance takes flight,
The world reveals its hidden light.

Through tangled paths, we roam, we find,
Each fleeting glimpse, a love so kind.
In every twist, our souls ignite,
In the chase of dreams, we take delight.

The search may wander from set design,
But serendipity leads us to align.
With every heartbeat, every turn,
In this dance of fate, we laugh and learn.

Chronicles of the Hidden Map

In ancient scrolls where stories dwell,
Chronicles whisper their arcane spell.
A hidden map engraved with lore,
Calls forth the brave to seek and explore.

Through deserts vast and mountains high,
Mysteries beckon beneath the sky.
Each mark a journey, each line a key,
Unlocking realms of what will be.

With lanterns bright, the seekers tread,
In search of treasures the dreamers spread.
The path unfolds, both wild and grand,
Guided by fate's unseen hand.

Each chapter written in stars above,
The whispers of courage, the echoes of love.
In chronicles old, our stories blend,
The hidden map leads us to the end.

Unveiling the Veil of Secrets

In shadows deep, where whispers dwell,
A hidden truth begins to swell.
With every step, the veil grows thin,
Revealing tales of loss and sin.

The sighing winds, they softly speak,
Of ancient dreams and futures bleak.
Each secret shared, a fleeting spark,
Illuminates the endless dark.

With cautious hearts, we tread the way,
Unveiling night, embracing day.
The mysteries fade, like morning mist,
Forever lost, yet still we persist.

Beneath the surface, shadows play,
The veil of secrets fades away.
In every truth, a lesson learned,
In every flame, a passion burned.

The Quest Beyond the Known

Upon the path where few have tread,
The quest for truth, a hunger fed.
Each step a question, every glance,
Invites the mind to dream and dance.

The stars above, a guiding light,
They urge us onward into night.
With hearts ablaze, we seek to find,
The wisdom shared by humankind.

Beyond the hills, where shadows creep,
Lies hidden knowledge, secrets deep.
With courage strong, we push ahead,
In search of answers, brave; not dread.

The journey's long, the road is wide,
Yet in the unknown, we confide.
For in the quest, our souls will grow,
And lead us to what's yet to show.

Nightfall in the Valley of Whispers

The sun descends, the darkness calls,
As twilight drapes, the shadow falls.
In the valley, soft voices sigh,
Underneath the velvet sky.

The leaves rustle, secrets shared,
Within the night, dreams are bared.
Each whisper hints at tales untold,
Of love, of loss, of courage bold.

Stars awaken, twinkle bright,
As echoes dance in the fading light.
The valley holds its breath in peace,
A sanctuary where worries cease.

In shades of blue, the world turns slow,
Restful souls let their thoughts flow.
Nightfall here, a gentle spell,
In the valley, all is well.

The Quest for the Unseen Treasure

Beneath the earth, where shadows lay,
A treasure waits, though far away.
With maps in hand, we seek the prize,
That glimmers bright beyond the skies.

Through tangled woods and rushing streams,
We chase the fragments of our dreams.
The thrill of search ignites our soul,
In every challenge, we feel whole.

Guided by fate, we conquer fears,
With every step, we shed our tears.
The unseen treasure lies within,
A journey rich, where hopes begin.

As time unfolds, the path reveals,
The truth transcends, the heart it heals.
The greatest treasure we can find,
Is love and courage intertwined.

The Enigma of the Elusive Route

Lost in the whispers of the breeze,
Twists and turns that aim to tease.
Footprints hidden in the sand,
Guided by the unseen hand.

Mysteries wrapped in shadowed light,
Path unfolds in the dead of night.
Every choice a game of chance,
Step by step in a timeless dance.

Flickers of the Celestial Pursuit

Stars align in a cosmic chase,
Each one holds a gleaming trace.
Through the vast and endless sea,
They beckon softly, calling me.

Wanderlust within my heart,
Fleeting moments that soon depart.
Mapping dreams in the darkened skies,
With every twinkle, a new surprise.

Wayfarers in the Realm of Dreams

In the hush where visions bloom,
Wayfarers tread on paths of gloom.
Chasing echoes of what once was,
As time folds gently, without pause.

Memories weave through misty air,
In the stillness, a whispered prayer.
Finding solace in the unknown,
A journey carved yet still unshown.

Explorers of the Endless Horizon

Beneath the sun where shadows play,
Explorers forge their daring way.
Chasing dreams that never tire,
With hearts ablaze, a fierce desire.

Mountains rise and rivers flow,
Endless stories waiting to show.
Nature sings in vibrant hues,
Horizon calls with a whispered muse.

Trials of the Lost Wanderers

In shadows deep, where silence reigns,
The wanderers roam through endless plains.
With heavy hearts and weary feet,
They chase the dawn, their dreams repeat.

Through tangled woods and rising fog,
They seek a sign, a guiding cog.
Each path they tread, a tale unfolds,
Of wandering souls and secrets told.

The stars above, their only guide,
In midnight skies, their fears they bide.
With every step, a chance to find,
The strength within, the ties that bind.

They journey on, through night and day,
As hope ignites the darkest way.
For every trial, a lesson learned,
In wanderlust, their hearts have burned.

Murmurs from the Hidden Realm

In twilight's hush, whispers arise,
From realms unseen, beneath the skies.
The echoes call with voices low,
To those who seek what lies below.

A garden blooms where shadows play,
In secret glades, the fae hold sway.
Their laughter lingers in the breeze,
A melody that brings unease.

With moonlight's touch, the path is clear,
To realms where magic draws near.
In every sigh, a tale is spun,
Of ancient dreams and things undone.

So listen close, and you might hear,
The whispered truths that thrill and sear.
The hidden realm, where wonders dwell,
Calls forth the brave, and casts its spell.

The Alluring Call of the Unexplored

Beyond the hills, where wild winds blow,
Lies an unknown land, a dream to show.
With every dawn that breaks anew,
Adventure calls; it beckons true.

The rivers murmur, rocks stand strong,
They sing of journeys, deep and long.
With open hearts and spirits free,
We yearn to touch infinity.

Through ancient woods and mountains high,
We chase the sun, beneath the sky.
The call of stars ignites the soul,
A quest to find what makes us whole.

In every step, the thrill resides,
The unexplored, where passion guides.
We'll chase the edges of the charts,
To find the beat of wandering hearts.

Charts of Chasing Whispers

Mapped in dreams, the whispers call,
From distant shores to skies that fall.
Each line a story, yet untold,
A journey vast, a heart so bold.

With every mark, a chance unfolds,
To seek the truth, the dreams of old.
The compass spins, the stars align,
In chasing whispers, hope will shine.

Through uncharted seas, we sail afar,
Guided by light from a distant star.
Each wave that crashes tells a tale,
Of daring souls that will not pale.

So take the charts, our map of chance,
In every whisper, join the dance.
For chasing dreams, in twilight's glow,
Will lead us where the wild winds flow.

Whims of the Wandering Souls

In the quiet night, stars whisper low,
Dreams afloat, where wild rivers flow.
Echoes of laughter blend with the breeze,
Wandering souls roam, seeking their ease.

Each path they wander, a story untold,
Treasures of memories, shimmering gold.
Footprints in sand, washed clear by the tide,
An endless adventure, where hearts coincide.

Journeys into the Unwritten

Pages unwritten, await the brave,
Each step a promise, each breath a wave.
Mountains loom tall, skies painted blue,
Guided by dreams, on paths forged anew.

Footsteps in silence, whispers of fate,
Winds carry secrets, never too late.
The compass of heart points to the unknown,
In every still moment, a seed has been sown.

Confessions of an Adventurer's Heart

With every heartbeat, a tale is spun,
Chasing horizons, where stories run.
In the depths of forests, or skies of grey,
An adventurer's spirit refuses to sway.

Unfolding horizons, my canvas of dreams,
Rivers of heartache, bursting at seams.
Each journey a brushstroke, bold and stark,
Crafting a mural, a life to embark.

Visions of the Untamed Frontier

Vast lands stretch forth, untouched and wild,
Calling the dreamers, the reckless and mild.
Mountains rise fiercely, shadows do play,
The spirit of nature, whispers, obey.

Chasing the sunset, we dance with the night,
In the wild embrace, everything feels right.
Stars are our guide, in the wilderness grand,
A journey continued, in an untamed land.

Interwoven Threads of Mystery

In shadows cast by ancient trees,
Whispers dance upon the breeze.
Threads of fate begin to weave,
Stories hidden, hard to believe.

Glimmers of truth in the night,
Flickering softly, just out of sight.
Each secret locked, yet so profound,
In the silence, mysteries abound.

With every turn and playful glance,
Life presents a curious chance.
Interwoven paths we tread,
A tapestry of thoughts unsaid.

Unraveling what lies beneath,
We seek the wisdom in belief.
In the dark, the light will show,
Threads of mystery ebb and flow.

Echoing Legends of the Unexplored

Beneath the stars, the stories grow,
Whispers of lands we yearn to know.
Legends echo through the sleek night,
Guiding adventurers with their light.

Each step taken, a tale begins,
In every heart, the spirit spins.
Uncharted realms, waiting in line,
Echo the dreams of olden time.

Mountains high and valleys low,
Every corner, secrets flow.
Mysteries cloaked in nature's grace,
Invite the wanderers to their place.

With courage found in wanderlust,
We chase the shadows, we chase the dust.
Echoing legends call us near,
To explore the world without fear.

The Portrait of a Wayward Dream

In colors bright, a vision gleams,
A canvas filled with wayward dreams.
Brushstrokes clash, yet harmonize,
Creating worlds of sweet surprise.

Figures dance in vibrant light,
Lost in the depth of the night.
Each portrait tells a tale untold,
Of hopes and dreams that dare be bold.

Fleeting moments captured still,
In the silence, echoes thrill.
Each gaze upon the painted face,
Whispers of longing, a soft embrace.

A wayward dream in colors spun,
A journey started, never done.
In every brush, a heartbeat lies,
The essence of life in art's disguise.

Navigating the Labyrinth of the Mind

A maze of thoughts, both wide and deep,
In winding paths, secrets keep.
Each turn unveils a shadowed truth,
The echoes of forgotten youth.

Whispers draw us near the brink,
In corridors where stillness sinks.
Questions drift like autumn leaves,
In the labyrinth, the spirit weaves.

Mirrors reflect the heart's desire,
Fleeting dreams ignite a fire.
Navigating twists with quiet grace,
Searching for a sacred place.

In the labyrinth of the mind,
Answers lost, yet joy's defined.
With every step, the journey flows,
In the echo of thoughts, the self grows.

Parables of the Pursuing Heart

In shadows deep, the heart does chase,
A whisper soft, a fleeting trace.
Through trials steep, it learns to soar,
Each beat ignites, forevermore.

With every step, a lesson learned,
In every flame, a passion burned.
A tapestry of love and loss,
In seeking truth, we bear the cross.

The road unwinds, a winding tale,
Through stormy seas, we will not fail.
A guiding star within us gleams,
In parables, we hold our dreams.

The heart, relentless, dares to seek,
In every whisper, hope shall speak.
Through darkened nights and brightened days,
The pursuing heart shall find its ways.

Songs of the Exploratory Spirits

In hidden paths where wonders bloom,
The restless souls find space to zoom.
With open hearts, they heed the call,
To soar above, to rise, to fall.

The mountain peaks, the valleys low,
In every step, a chance to grow.
Beneath the stars, they sing their tune,
Exploratory spirits, night and noon.

The ocean's waves, the forest's song,
In every place, they feel they belong.
With every breeze, and every flight,
They dance with shadows, chase the light.

Through paths untrodden, bold they roam,
In every journey, they find a home.
With open hearts and fearless might,
The exploratory spirits take their flight.

Dreams Out of Reach

Beneath the stars, desires dwell,
In silent whispers, hopes compel.
With every heartbeat, yearnings rise,
Unbroken threads that touch the skies.

Through forest dark and canyon deep,
In every shadow, secrets keep.
With longing hearts, we shoot for high,
Yet dreams may slip, as time goes by.

The distant shore, a fading light,
Each step we take draws us from sight.
In laughter sweet, in tears we stand,
The dreams we chase slip through our hand.

Yet still we dream, for hope remains,
In every loss, a spirit gains.
With every sigh, we find our reach,
In every heart, dreams softly teach.

The Enchantment of Wandering

In gentle winds, the wanderers roam,
Through fields of gold, they find their home.
With open eyes, they seek the new,
In every path, a world untrue.

The mountains call, the rivers flow,
In every step, they seek to know.
With each horizon, stories blend,
The enchantment of wandering knows no end.

Through ancient woods and cities bright,
Each corner turned reveals a light.
With curious hearts, they trace the skies,
In every gaze, the spirit flies.

The magic whispers, never still,
In every heart, a spark to thrill.
With every journey, they ignite,
The enchantment of wandering takes flight.

The Search for Forgotten Dreams

In shadows deep, where whispers dwell,
A spark of hope begins to swell.
Faded echoes of wishes lost,
A journey's worth, no matter the cost.

Through forests dense and mountains high,
We chase the stars across the sky.
Each step we take, a story unfolds,
In the heart, a flame that never grows cold.

With eyes wide open, we seek the night,
For every dream holds a hidden light.
In the silence, we hear the call,
Awakening a spirit that will not fall.

So let us wander, hand in hand,
In search of dreams, in distant lands.
With courage strong and hearts aglow,
We'll find the treasures time can't bestow.

Mysteries Wrapped in Time's Embrace

In a world where shadows play,
Time unveils what words can't say.
Each tick, a story yet untold,
Wrapped in layers of silence bold.

Moments linger, soft and rare,
Whispers of the past fill the air.
Lost in echoes, a secret rhyme,
A dance of ages, wrapped in time.

Beneath the stars, our fates entwine,
Unlocking doors with every sign.
In the stillness, mysteries gleam,
Life's true essence, a fragile dream.

So let us venture into the night,
Embrace the shadows, seek the light.
For in each heartbeat, a tale awaits,
In time's embrace, love never abates.

The Puzzle of the Wandering Soul

A restless heart, it roams afar,
Collecting pieces, like fallen stars.
Each fragment found along the road,
A hint of truth, in stories flowed.

In tranquil nights and bright moonlight,
The wandering soul seeks what feels right.
With every step, the pieces fit,
A tapestry of life, we carefully knit.

Questions linger, like whispers breeze,
In every moment, mysteries tease.
Through joy and sorrow, love and pain,
The puzzle grows, each loss a gain.

So let us wander, explore the whole,
Find the threads that bind the soul.
In the journey, our truth unfolds,
A beautiful mosaic, daring and bold.

Enchantment in Every Step

With every step upon the earth,
A dance of magic, a new rebirth.
Nature whispers secrets sweet,
In every corner, enchantments greet.

The sunlit path, the moonlit night,
Every shadow, a flicker of light.
In laughter shared and tears that fall,
Life’s true magic embraces us all.

As flowers bloom and rivers flow,
Each moment sparkles, a vibrant glow.
With open hearts, we roam and play,
Finding wonders in everyday.

So let us cherish this grand array,
The beauty hidden in each day.
For in our steps, both bold and meek,
Lies the enchantment that we seek.